W9-CSL-205

DOCUMENTING U.S. HISTORY

THE **ARTICLES** OF **CONFEDERATION**

Liz Sonneborn

Chicago, Illinois

www.capstonepub.com

Visit our website to find out more information about Heinemann-Raintree books.

To order:

 Phone 800-747-4992

Visit www.capstonepub.com to browse our catalog and order online.

Edited by Abby Colich, Megan Cotugno, and Laura Hensley
Designed by Cynthia Della-Rovere
Original illustrations © Capstone Global Library Limited 2011
Illustrated by Oxford Designers & Illustrators
Picture research by Tracy Cummins
Originated by Capstone Global Library Limited
Printed and bound in the United States of America in North Mankato, Minnesota.   032013   007187RP

16 15 14 13
10 9 8 7 6 5 4 3 2

Library of Congress Cataloging-in-Publication Data
Sonneborn, Liz.
  The Articles of Confederation / Liz Sonneborn.
    p. cm.—(Documenting U.S. history)
  Includes bibliographical references and index.
  ISBN 978-1-4329-6749-9 (hb)—ISBN 978-1-4329-6758-1 (pb) 1. United States. Articles of Confederation. 2. Constitutional history—United States. 3. United States—Politics and government—1775-1783. I. Title.
  KF4508.S66 2013
  342.7302'9—dc23   2011037709

Acknowledgments
The author and publishers are grateful to the following for permission to reproduce copyright material: Alamy: pp. 18 (© Philip Scalia), 29 (© North Wind Picture Archives); Corbis: pp. 9 (© Bettmann), 15 (© Burstein Collection), 32 (© Bettmann); Getty Images: pp. 5 (KAREN BLEIER/AFP), 23 (Sarah L. Voisin/The Washington), 25 (MPI), 34 (Superstock), 37 (Jeff J Mitchell), 38 (MIGUEL GUTIERREZ/AFP), 43 (PAUL J. RICHARDS/AFP); Library of Congress Prints and Photographs Division: pp. 11, 14, 16, 19, 21, 28, 30, 31, 33; National Archives: pp. 13, 35, 40, 41; North Wind Picture Archives: p. 24 (© North Wind); Shutterstock: pp. 6 (© Galina Mikhalishina), 10 (© Tom Grundy), 12 (© John Kropewnicki); The Granger Collection: pp. 17, 26.

Cover image of Samuel Adams reproduced with permission from Getty Images (Stock Montage/Stock Montage). Cover image of John Dickinson reproduced with permission from Alamy (© North Wind Picture Archives). Cover image of the Articles of Confederation reproduced with permission from the National Archives (Charters of Freedom).

Every effort has been made to contact copyright holders of material reproduced in this book. Any omissions will be rectified in subsequent printings if notice is given to the publisher.

Contents

Some words are printed in **bold**, like this. You can find out what they mean by looking in the glossary.

Studying Documents

Throughout history, people have left records of events that happened to them. These records are called **primary sources**. They are important tools that historians use to learn about the past.

Official papers

Some primary sources are official papers. These documents might describe how a government works or explain laws it has passed. Officials who write these documents choose their words carefully. They want to make sure that anyone who reads them understands exactly what they are meant to say.

There are many important documents in U.S. history. One of the earliest was the **Articles** of **Confederation**. This document set out rules for the first government of the United States.

Newspapers, letters, and diaries

Other types of written primary sources include newspaper and magazine articles from the time. By studying these, historians can get an idea about what people thought about the news of the day. Sources like letters and diaries also provide interesting facts about earlier time periods. They help historians understand what ordinary people thought about their lives and times.

Primary sources not only offer information. They also provide an emotional tie to people who lived long ago. It is hard to look at an old handwritten letter and not wonder about the person who wrote it.

At many museums, visitors can learn about the past by viewing documents and other primary sources.

Other primary sources

Primary sources are not always written materials. They may be photographs, maps, recordings, or films. Historians sometimes even study everyday objects, such as tools, furniture, and works of art. These items allow historians to gather clues about how people used to live. Old toys, for instance, can help them discover how children used to play.

Protecting documents

Many important primary sources are found in museums and **archives**. There, experts store the items carefully so they do not get damaged. Experts have to be especially careful with items made of paper. Not only can documents be easily torn and wrinkled. The paper, if exposed to too much sunlight or moisture, can also fall apart over time.

Some of the most important documents in U.S. history are stored in two places in Washington, D.C. The National Archives collects important government documents. The Library of **Congress** holds more than 147 million items. These include documents, books, maps, and photographs.

In addition to books, many important documents are stored at the Library of Congress.

Secondary sources

Studying primary sources is not the only way to learn about the past. People can also read books, textbooks, encyclopedia articles, and other materials written by experts on other time periods. These are called **secondary sources**. People who write secondary sources study many primary sources and use what they learn to create a complete picture of a period of time or event. This book, for instance, is a secondary source.

The best way to understand a historical event is to use both primary and secondary sources. Primary sources allow you to imagine how people in the past felt and thought about their lives. Secondary sources help you make sense of primary sources by explaining their place in history.

The Fight for Independence

The document called the **Articles** of **Confederation** was written during the **Revolutionary War** (1775–1783). This war was fought between the **colonial** and British armies, mostly in what is now the eastern United States.

Protesting British rule

Before the Revolutionary War, American **colonists** lived in 13 **colonies**. The colonies were ruled by the government of Great Britain. The colonists were governed by the British government.

As time went by, the colonists grew unhappy with British rule. They were especially upset by the high taxes they were forced to pay to the British government. Every time the colonists bought certain goods, such as paper products or tea, they had to pay a tax.

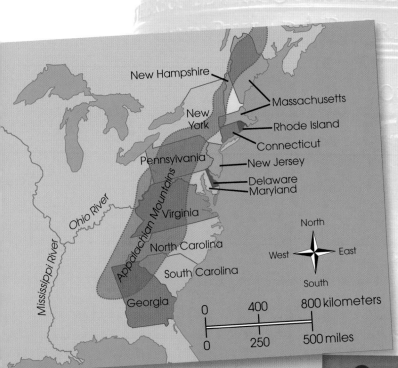

This map shows the original 13 colonies that existed before the Revolutionary War.

May 14, 1607
Colonists found Jamestown, the first permanent British settlement in what is now the United States.

Many colonists thought these taxes were unfair. Some protested against the British government. One such protest was held in Boston, Massachusetts. There, angry colonists threw crates of tea into the waters of Boston Harbor. The protest became known as the Boston Tea Party. By this time, many colonists had come to think of themselves more as American than as British.

During the Boston Tea Party, colonists, dressed like American Indians, protested the taxes the British placed on tea.

December 16, 1773
Colonists protest British taxes at the Boston Tea Party.

The First Continental Congress

Colonial leaders decided they had to take action. In September 1774, **delegates** from the 13 colonies gathered together in Philadelphia, Pennsylvania. There, they formed the First Continental **Congress**. During this meeting, the delegates talked about what they should do about their problems with the British.

Some leaders decided to send a message to the British king, George III (see box on page 11). In the message, they laid out all their complaints. But King George did nothing to improve the situation.

The building in Philadelphia where the Continental Congress met was later named Independence Hall.

Know It!

The members of the Continental Congress all took an oath of secrecy. They swore not to tell anyone what they discussed. They wanted to make sure the British did not know any details about their meetings.

September 1774
The First Continental Congress meets in Philadelphia.

The first shots of the Revolutionary War were fired during the battles of Lexington and Concord.

The tensions between the colonists and the British continued to grow. Finally, in the spring of 1775, the two sides met on the battlefield. At the Massachusetts towns of Lexington and Concord, the colonists exchanged gunfire with the British Army. These battles marked the beginning of a conflict that became known as the Revolutionary War.

George III (1738–1820)

George III became king of Great Britain when he was just 22 years old. The Revolutionary War occurred while he was on the throne. In the **Declaration** of Independence, colonial leaders said King George had "plundered our seas, ravaged our Coasts, burnt our towns, and destroyed the Lives of our people."

April 19, 1775
The Battles of Lexington and Concord mark the beginning of the Revolutionary War.

The Need for Government

A month later, the Continental **Congress** met for a second time. Richard Henry Lee, a **delegate** from Virginia, proposed that the delegates make a "plan of **confederation**."

Lee's proposal

The **colonies**, which were now called states, each had their own separate governments. But, Lee said, they also needed to join together under a national government. Such a government would be able to set down rules that all the states had to follow.

There were several good reasons to do this. A well-organized national government could help them manage the war properly. It could also raise money for the troops, recruit new soldiers, and transport supplies for the army.

Drafting the Articles of Confederation

York Town, Pennsylvania 1777 13 USA c.

This U.S. postage stamp was issued in 1977, 200 years after Congress approved the **Articles of Confederation.**

May 10, 1775
The Second Continental Congress begins meeting in Philadelphia.

A strong national government

Colonial leaders had still more arguments in favor of forming a national government. They hoped to persuade foreign countries to support their cause. These countries might have more confidence that the American **colonists** could beat the British if the Americans had their own solid, national government. If the Americans won the war, they would also need a national government in place to help run their new country.

Still, some delegates were not so sure about Lee's idea. They did not want a strong national government. If it was too powerful, they feared Americans would feel no freer than they had felt under British rule.

Americans celebrate the day the Declaration of Independence was *ratified* every Fourth of July.

June 7, 1776
Richard Henry Lee proposes that the delegates of the Continental Congress make a "plan of confederation."

The Confederation Committee

Despite these concerns, the Second Continental Congress formed a committee on June 11, 1776. The Confederation Committee was charged with writing a plan for a new government that would bind the states together. It included one delegate from each state.

The delegates chose John Dickinson from Pennsylvania to be the committee chairman. He brought to its meetings a copy of an earlier plan for confederation **drafted** by Benjamin Franklin, one of the most respected colonial leaders. In 1775 the Continental Congress had discussed the plan, but the delegates had chosen not to act on it.

Years earlier, Franklin had presented yet another plan to unite the colonies, at the Albany Congress of 1754. The delegates to that **conference** approved Franklin's proposal. But the individual colonies rejected it. The colonies were suspicious and often jealous of one another. They did not then see the value of working closely together.

Benjamin Franklin first proposed a central government for the American colonies in the 1750s.

June 11, 1776
The Second Continental Congress forms a committee to draw up a plan for confederation.

14

Declaring independence

Also during the Second Continental Congress, Lee made a speech. He said that the colonies should declare themselves free from British rule. The others agreed and chose a young delegate named Thomas Jefferson (see the box) to draft the **declaration**.

On July 4, 1776, the members of the Continental Congress ratified Jefferson's Declaration of Independence. It stated that the colonies were now independent of Great Britain.

Thomas Jefferson (1743–1826)

A planter from Virginia, Thomas Jefferson was only 33 years old when he wrote the Declaration of Independence. He was elected the second governor of the state of Virginia in 1779 and the third president of the United States in 1800. After leaving the presidency, Jefferson worked to establish the University of Virginia.

July 4, 1776
The Continental Congress ratifies the Declaration of Independence.

Drafting the Articles

As they worked on their plan for a national government, members of the **Confederation** Committee remembered the failure of past plans. The committee knew that each state had its own concerns and priorities. State leaders saw themselves as serving their states first. They would resist a central government that did not allow their states to conduct their own affairs as they saw fit.

The first draft

With this in mind, the committee got to work. Within a month, it had a **draft** of a confederation plan. Chairman John Dickinson (see the box) had written most of it. The document was entitled "**Articles** of Confederation and Perpetual Union."

Charles Thomson was secretary of the Continental Congress throughout its entire existence.

July 12, 1776
The Confederation Committee presents the Continental Congress with a draft of the Articles of Confederation.

John Dickinson
(1732–1808)

Before the **Revolutionary War**, John Dickinson wrote many newspaper articles that criticized high British taxes. Still, he was opposed to going to war with Britain. He refused to sign the **Declaration** of Independence, although he did serve in the **colonial** army. In addition to writing most of the Articles of Confederation, Dickinson later also helped draft the U.S. **Constitution**.

The Articles of Confederation, as it became known, was presented to the Continental **Congress**. Charles Thomson, the secretary of the Congress, then had 80 copies printed. He gave one copy to each **delegate**.

In July and August 1776, Congress debated the Articles. Thomson took notes on the talks. He then revised, or updated, the document and printed 80 new copies.

The delegates' discussion of the Articles of Confederation was far from over. But they had to put the matter aside. They had to focus on winning the war against the British.

July–August 1776
The Continental Congress debates the Articles of Confederation.

Escaping the British Army

In late 1777, the Continental Congress received some alarming news. British troops were closing in on Philadelphia. To escape the British, the delegates fled from the city. They headed west to York County, Pennsylvania. There, the delegates felt safe enough to get back to work. Meeting in the county's courthouse, they again started to discuss the Articles of Confederation.

In late 1777, the Continental Congress began meeting in the York County Courthouse in Pennsylvania.

Questions about the Articles

The Congress had to deal with several big questions. One was about how strong the national government should be. Most states did not want to give up any of their power. They believed their state legislators, or lawmakers, knew best how to govern their states. States in the South were especially concerned. There, **slavery** was legal. Those southern states feared the new national government would try to outlaw slavery.

September 1777
The Continental Congress is forced to move from Philadelphia before British soldiers enter the city. The Congress moves to York County, Pennsylvania, to meet.

Another question concerned the number of votes each state should have in the new government. States with large populations thought they should have more votes than states with smaller ones. States with small populations, however, believed all states should have an equal say.

After much arguing, on November 15, 1777, the Congress approved a version of the Articles of Confederation. No one in Congress thought the document was perfect. But most thought it was better than no government at all.

Samuel Adams
(1722–1803)

Samuel Adams served on the Confederation Committee, representing Massachusetts. A strong supporter of the Revolutionary War, he was known for his fiery speeches. Adams's second cousin, John Adams, later served as the second president of the United States.

November 15, 1777
The Continental Congress approves the Articles of Confederation.

Seeking ratification

The Continental Congress printed copies of the latest version of the Articles of Confederation. They sent these copies to every state **legislature**. With the documents, Congress sent instructions to each state to **ratify**, or approve, the Articles as soon as possible.

By early July 1778, eight states had ratified the document. But Congress had decided that the Articles had to be approved by all 13 states. Getting the other five states on board took far longer than anyone expected.

Western land claims

Slowly, four of the five states ratified the Articles. But still one withheld approval—Maryland. The reason why had to do with an area of land west of the 13 states (see the map on page 27). This area stretched from the Appalachian Mountains to the Mississippi River. Several states, including Virginia and New York, claimed part of this land. If the national government approved their claims, these states would become very big.

November 28, 1777
Congressional delegates receive copies of the Articles of Confederation to take to their state legislatures.

Maryland, a smaller state with fixed borders, feared the power such big states would have. Maryland's **representatives** insisted that Virginia and New York give up their land claims and allow Congress to control the western territory.

Maryland refused to back down. For the good of the new nation, New York gave up its western land. Finally, Maryland agreed to ratify the Articles of Confederation. On March 1, 1781, the Articles became the law of the land.

This version of the Articles of Confederation, printed in 1777, was sent to the states for ratification.

March 1, 1781
The Articles of Confederation go into effect.

ARTICLES

OF

Confederatio

AND

Perpetual Unio

BETWEEN THE

STATE

OF

NEW HAMPSHIRE, MASSACHUSETTS BAY, RHODE ISLAND, AND PROVIDENCE PLA
CONNECTICUT, NEW YORK, NEW JERSEY, PENNSYLVANIA, DELAWARE, N
VIRGINIA, NORTH CAROLINA, SOUTH CAROLINA, AND GEORGIA.

WILLIAMSB
Printed by ALEXANDER PURD

The Articles in Action

The **ratified** copy of the **Articles** of **Confederation** began with a **preamble**, or introduction. It said that all the states had agreed to everything in the document. It was followed by 13 articles. These sections explained how the new national government would be set up. At the end was a conclusion, below which the members of **Congress** signed their names.

A new Congress

According to the Articles, the structure of the national government was simple. It would include only one body, Congress. This Confederation Congress was responsible for making decisions about matters that affected all of the states.

"For the most convenient management of the general interests of the United States, delegates shall be annually [yearly] appointed in such manner as the legislatures of each State shall direct, to meet in Congress on the first Monday in November, in every year."

—*from Article V of the Articles of Confederation*

Under the Articles of Confederation, Congress selected one member to serve as its president. This official, however, had little real power. John Hanson of Maryland was the first president of the Confederation Congress. Some historians say that he—not George Washington—was really the first president of the United States.

Each year, a state **legislature** would appoint its state's **delegates** to Congress. Each delegate served a one-year term. States could send anywhere from two to seven **representatives** to Congress each year. But no matter how many delegates a state had, the state could only cast one vote. Whenever a law was proposed, all of a state's representatives had to agree to vote either for it or against it.

This statue shows John Hanson, who served as the first president of Congress under the Articles of Confederation.

Powers of the national government

The Articles of Confederation assigned several powers to the new national government, which was the Congress:

The Confederation government was charged with operating a national postal service. In the days before telephones and computers, people relied on letters that were delivered on horseback during the early days of the United States.

- Only Congress could declare war or make peace with a foreign country.

- Congress was also in charge of the country's army and navy.

- Congress was allowed to borrow money and to settle boundary disputes between states.

- Congress was responsible for signing **treaties** and dealing with American Indian groups.

- Congress would run the national post office.

At the same time, the document placed limits on the national government's authority. For instance, regulating (controlling) trade and all other matters related to buying and selling goods fell to the states.

Even more importantly, the national government had little power to raise money. It could ask states for money, but it could not force them to pay taxes.

The Articles of Confederation also made it difficult to pass national laws. It required that 9 of the 13 states agree to any important piece of legislation (laws). Changing the Articles was even harder. Any **amendment**, or change, to the Articles required approval by all 13 states.

"The United States in Congress assembled, shall have the sole and exclusive right and power of determining on peace and war...of sending and receiving ambassadors [representatives from other countries] [and of] entering into treaties and alliances."

—*from Article IX of the Articles of Confederation*

The Articles of Confederation gave the national government responsibility for all official dealings with American Indian groups.

Reconsidering the Confederation

In a few ways, the **Confederation** government was a success. Its ability to organize the states helped the U.S. Army win the final stages of the **Revolutionary War**. The fighting stopped in October 1781.

But it took almost two more years for the United States and Great Britain to negotiate peace. The peace **treaty**—the Treaty of Paris of 1783—was another accomplishment of the Confederation **Congress**.

The Confederation government could issue coins, but not banknotes (paper money). Many states printed their own money.

Dealing with western lands

Now that the United States had won its independence, Congress could take up another important issue. Its leaders began to think about the western land controlled by the national government. Congress made a series of laws dealing with the area, which was called the Northwest Territory (see the map). The most important was the Northwest Ordinance of 1787. It set down rules for how to divide the land and form it into states.

October 17, 1781
The fighting during the Revolutionary War ends with the British surrender at Yorktown.

September 3, 1783
The United States signs the Treaty of Paris, which formally ends the Revolutionary War.

Congress formed five states out of the Northwest Territory.

Problems arise

Despite these successes, from the start, there were problems with the **Articles** of Confederation. The Confederation government did not have much power. For example, the national government could not settle disputes between states. As a result, state **legislatures** thought they could do whatever they wanted. If the national government passed a law they did not like, state legislatures just ignored it. They knew the Confederation government could not force them to obey.

"Each state retains [keeps] its sovereignty [authority to govern itself], freedom, and independence, and every power, jurisdiction [power to make legal decisions], and right, which is not by this Confederation expressly delegated to the United States, in Congress assembled."

—*from Article II of the Articles of Confederation*

May 20, 1785
The Land Ordinance of 1785 allows Congress to raise money by selling western land.

Debt and trade trouble

The states also often refused to give the Confederation government money. This was a huge problem for the new U.S. government. The government was deeply in debt, because it had borrowed money to fight the Revolutionary War.

The government also could not control trade between states or with other countries. This problem affected everyday people. With unregulated (uncontrolled) trade, prices for food and other goods began to rise. People also had trouble finding jobs.

In the 1800s, all kinds of goods were bought and sold at U.S. ports.

Rebellion leader Daniel Shays, once a captain in the colonial army, was angry that the national government had not given soldiers the pay it owed them.

Shays's Rebellion

The bad economic times made many Americans angry. A group of farmers in Massachusetts was especially upset. They were in danger of losing their farms because they could not pay their rent. A local leader named Daniel Shays led several hundred farmers in a protest. They surrounded the courthouse in Springfield. They then attacked the place where a stash of weapons was stored. The protest was called Shays's Rebellion.

The rebellion frightened many leaders in Congress. They were afraid other angry Americans would soon rise up. If they did, the congressmen wondered if the United States would survive.

January 25, 1787
Poor farmers in Massachusetts rise up during Shays's Rebellion.

The Annapolis Convention

One U.S. leader who was particularly concerned about these problems was James Madison (see box on page 31). He was a young congressman from Virginia. Virginia and neighboring Maryland were having a heated trade dispute, which the national government did not have the power to settle.

(see box on page 31)

*In 1786, 12 **delegates** from five states met at the Annapolis State House intending to talk about how to solve trade disputes.*

Madison used the situation to organize a **conference** to discuss trade issues. Madison invited all the states to send **representatives** to the meeting. It was held in Annapolis, Maryland.

Leaders from only five states bothered to come. Instead of talking about trade, they discussed the Articles of Confederation.

James Madison
(1751–1836)

In 1780, 29-year-old James Madison, from Virginia, became the youngest member of the Continental Congress. Seven years later, he helped write the U.S. **Constitution**, which replaced the Articles of Confederation. In 1809, Madison became the fourth U.S. president.

Everyone agreed that the Confederation government was not working well. They wanted to rewrite the document to create a stronger national government.

Alexander Hamilton, a young congressman from New York, attended the Annapolis Convention. Afterward, he wrote up a report about it, which was sent to Congress. Hamilton called on Congress to take action. He declared it was time for the United States to create a new and improved plan for its government.

September 11, 1786
State representatives discuss the limitations of the Articles of Confederation at the Annapolis Convention.

From Articles to Constitution

Hamilton's report inspired **Congress** to organize the Philadelphia **Conference** of 1787. (Today, this meeting is better known as the Constitutional **Convention**.) Twelve states sent 55 **delegates** to the meeting. Rhode Island was the only state not represented.

Getting rid of the Articles

The delegates were supposed to suggest changes to the **Articles** of **Confederation**. But almost immediately, they saw this was not enough. Instead of changing the Articles, they decided to get rid of the document altogether. The delegates wanted an entirely new plan for the national government.

The delegates at the Constitutional Convention included John Dickinson, Alexander Hamilton, James Madison, and Benjamin Franklin, among others.

Alexander Hamilton
(1757–1804)

While still a teenager, Alexander Hamilton joined the **colonial** army and fought in several battles of the **Revolutionary War**. He was later elected to Congress and helped **draft** the U.S. Constitution. In 1789 Hamilton became the first secretary of the treasury. While serving as governor of New York, Hamilton was killed in a duel in 1804.

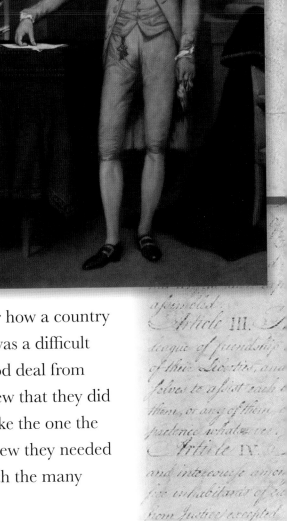

The delegates at the Constitutional Convention set out to write a **constitution** for the United States. A constitution is a set of rules for how a country is governed. Drafting the Constitution was a difficult job. But the delegates had learned a good deal from the Articles of Confederation. They knew that they did not want a weak national government like the one the Articles provided. The delegates now knew they needed a government strong enough to deal with the many problems the United States was facing.

May–September 1787
The Philadelphia Conference—now known as the Constitutional Convention—meets.

Three branches

Under the Articles of Confederation, the only government body was Congress. Under the new constitution, the national government was larger. Its various bodies were also divided into three separate branches—the legislative, the judicial, and the executive.

In the Constitution, Congress fell under the legislative branch. But this Congress was different from the Congress of the Articles of Confederation. It was made up of two houses—the House of **Representatives** and the Senate—instead of one. Also, house members (and later senators) were elected directly by the citizens of each state.

The two other branches were completely new additions to the national government. The judicial branch was responsible for enforcing laws. The executive branch, which included the president, was charged with running the government.

Future president George Washington led the Constitutional Convention.

September 17, 1787
A draft of the new Constitution is sent to the states to be ratified.

June 21, 1788
The U.S. Constitution is ratified by nine states.

Like the authors of the Articles of Confederation, the delegates were concerned about a national government with too much power. In response to this concern, the authors of the Articles had made the government fairly weak. The writers of the Constitution came up with a different solution. They spread power across the three branches of the government. That way, no one government body could become too powerful.

Amending the Constitution

The drafters of the Constitution also recognized that the Articles of Confederation had been too difficult to change. They decided that only two-thirds of the states had to approve **amendments** to the new constitution.

Today, the U.S. Constitution includes 27 amendments.

On June 21, 1788, the U.S. Constitution was **ratified** by nine states. On March 4, 1789, it went into effect. The Articles of Confederation became part of history.

March 4, 1789
The U.S. Constitution goes into effect.

Preserving the Past

Most of the earliest copies of the **Articles** of **Confederation** have been lost. But a few survive.

Surviving copies

Among the surviving copes is the **engrossed** version. **Congress** had this official copy made in June 1778. The engrossed copy was handwritten on **parchment**, which is animal skin that has been scraped of fur and stretched. The Articles were written in ink using a fancy style of script.

Other surviving versions were printed. Two of them include handwritten notes in the margins. Congressmen wrote these notes when they were discussing the Articles. These notes make these two copies especially valuable. They have allowed historians to piece together what the congressmen talked about during those discussions.

Know It!

When the Articles of Confederation was written, there were only a few ways to create a document. A document could be written by hand or set in type by a professional printer. Today, people still handwrite and print documents. But they also make documents in new ways. For instance, they can type a document using a computer and save it as a computer file. To make a paper copy, all they have to do is print it out on their personal printer.

*The work of preserving important old documents falls to trained experts called **conservators**.*

Protecting original documents

It is no accident that those copies of the Articles survived. They would have fallen apart had they not been protected in **archives**. Archives are places that collect historical documents and records. In archives, documents are carefully stored and preserved so that future generations can see them.

Archivists at work

People who work in archives are called **archivists**. They are professionally trained in properly storing all types of materials. Sometimes an archive might receive a document that has been soiled or damaged. Archivists then ask conservators for help. Conservators know ways to repair documents and other objects. A good conservator can make an old document look almost like it did when it was first written.

Archivists also keep detailed records of everything in their archive. This way if a visitor wants to see a particular item, the archivist can find it quickly.

Archivists help historians and other people research topics of interest to them.

Solving mysteries

The history behind a very famous document like the Articles of Confederation is easy to find. But often an archive might receive items about which little is known. For instance, an archivist might have a pile of old letters, but have no idea who wrote them.

An archivist then must become a detective. By studying various **primary sources** and **secondary sources**, an archivist tries to piece together information about mysterious objects.

Serving the public

Another job of archivists is sharing what they learn with the public. They often choose particularly interesting objects and place them on display. They also might write explanations of these objects so visitors can understand them better.

Know It!

Many people are interested in learning about their ancestors— relatives who lived a long time ago. At archives, they can often find the information they need to trace their family tree through history.

The Articles of Confederation Today

The original **engrossed** copy of the **Articles** of **Confederation** is now stored in the National **Archives** in Washington, D.C. The National Archives is also home to the original versions of the **Declaration** of Independence and the U.S. **Constitution**. These documents are in a permanent display called the Charters of Freedom. Visitors can view them anytime.

Protecting the Articles

The National Archives only displays the Articles of Confederation from time to time. When it is not displayed, the document is carefully stored so that it will not be damaged. It is placed flat in a folder inside a box. The box protects the Articles from light, but it allows air to circulate around the document. The area where it is stored is kept cool. The air there is also very dry because humidity (moisture in the air) can damage **parchment**.

The Charters of Freedom exhibit at the National Archives displays the Declaration of Independence and the Constitution.

For as old as it is, the Articles of Confederation is in fairly good shape. But it does show some wear and tear around the edges. This suggests that at some time in its history, the document was rolled up before being stored.

The engrossed copy of the Articles of Confederation is carefully preserved in the National Archives.

The Articles' importance

Why does the National Archives go to such lengths to preserve the Articles of Confederation? After all, in comparison to the U.S. Constitution, it does not seem very important. The Constitution set down the rules by which the U.S. government still operates today. The Articles, on the other hand, describes a government that was abandoned more than 200 years ago.

The Articles in history

One answer is that the Articles of Confederation has a bigger place in U.S. history than it might seem at first glance. It was written by many of the people who worked and fought hardest to make the United States an independent nation. Its words reveal what these **Founding Fathers** thought was important when the country was young.

The Articles of Confederation also helps show why the U.S. Constitution was written. Many U.S. leaders quickly saw the flaws of the confederation and realized they needed a new type of government. The story of the U.S. Constitution, then, begins with the Articles of Confederation.

The Articles of Confederation also helps create a personal connection with the Founding Fathers who wrote it so long ago. In history books, they seem like larger-than-life figures. But their signatures on the Articles remind us that the Founding Fathers were just human beings. Realizing that only makes their struggles to create the United States seem all the more impressive.

Under the United States Constitution, three branches of government work together to run the country. In this photograph, President George W. Bush, head of the executive branch, addresses Congress, the legislative branch.

Timeline

May 14, 1607
Colonists found Jamestown, the first permanent settlement in what is now the United States.

December 16, 1773
Colonists protest British taxes at the Boston Tea Party.

September 1774
The First Continental Congress meets in Philadelphia.

July 12, 1776
The Confederation Committee presents the Continental Congress with a draft of the Articles of Confederation.

July 4, 1776
The Continental Congress ratifies the Declaration of Independence.

July–August 1776
The Continental Congress debates the Articles of Confederation.

September 1777
The Continental Congress is forced to move from Philadelphia before British soldiers enter the city. The Congress moves to York County, Pennsylvania, to meet.

September 11, 1786
State representatives discuss the limitations of the Articles of Confederation at the Annapolis Convention.

May 20, 1785
The Land Ordinance of 1785 allows Congress to raise money by selling western land.

January 25, 1787
Poor farmers in Massachusetts rise up during Shays's Rebellion.

May–September 1787
The Philadelphia Conference—now known as the Constitutional Convention—meets.

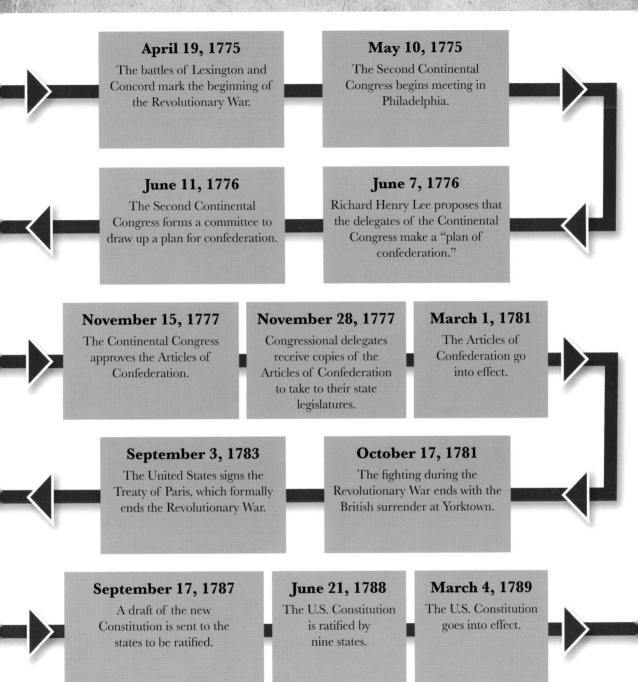

April 19, 1775

The battles of Lexington and Concord mark the beginning of the Revolutionary War.

May 10, 1775

The Second Continental Congress begins meeting in Philadelphia.

June 11, 1776

The Second Continental Congress forms a committee to draw up a plan for confederation.

June 7, 1776

Richard Henry Lee proposes that the delegates of the Continental Congress make a "plan of confederation."

November 15, 1777

The Continental Congress approves the Articles of Confederation.

November 28, 1777

Congressional delegates receive copies of the Articles of Confederation to take to their state legislatures.

March 1, 1781

The Articles of Confederation go into effect.

September 3, 1783

The United States signs the Treaty of Paris, which formally ends the Revolutionary War.

October 17, 1781

The fighting during the Revolutionary War ends with the British surrender at Yorktown.

September 17, 1787

A draft of the new Constitution is sent to the states to be ratified.

June 21, 1788

The U.S. Constitution is ratified by nine states.

March 4, 1789

The U.S. Constitution goes into effect.

Glossary

amendment change or addition to an official document

archive place that holds a collection of historical documents and other primary sources

archivist expert who works in an archive

article portion of an official or legal document

colonial having to do with a colony

colonist person who lives in a colony

colony area controlled by another country

confederation group of countries, states, or territories bound together in an alliance

conference formal meeting

congress formal meeting of a group

conservator expert who repairs and restores old documents

constitution written set of rules by which a government operates

convention large meeting

declaration formal announcement

delegate person sent to a meeting to represent others

draft early version of a document; also, to write such an early version

engross to create the final version of a legal document

Founding Father American leader who established the national government of the United States

legislature government body that makes laws

parchment thin paper-like material

preamble introduction

primary source document or object made in the past that provides information about a certain time

ratify approve

representative person chosen to speak for a larger group of people

Revolutionary War war fought by American colonists from 1775 to 1783 to win independence from British rule

secondary source account written by someone who studied primary sources

slavery practice of owning slaves

treaty formal agreement between countries

Find Out More

Books

Catel, Patrick. *Key People of the Revolutionary War*. Chicago: Heinemann Library, 2011.

Fleming, Thomas. *Everybody's Revolution*. New York: Scholastic, 2006.

Huey, Lois Miner. *Voices of the American Revolution*. Mankato, Minn.: Capstone, 2011.

Isaacs, Sally Senzell. *Understanding the Articles of Confederation*. New York: Crabtree, 2009.

Stein, R. Conrad. *The National Archives*. Danbury, Conn.: Franklin Watts, 2002.

Websites

http://history.state.gov/milestones/1776-1783/Articles
U.S. Department of State: Office of the Historian
This website explains the history of the Articles of Confederation.

www.loc.gov/rr/program/bib/ourdocs/articles.html
The Library of Congress: Primary Documents in American History
Visit this site for links to information about the Confederation government.

http://memory.loc.gov/ammem/collections/continental/intro01.html
The Library of Congress: To Form a More Perfect Union
This website describes the creation of the Articles of Confederation and the U.S. Constitution.

http://myloc.gov/Exhibitions/creatingtheus/Pages/default.aspx
The Library of Congress: Creating the United States
Visit this website to view images from the Library of Congress's Creating the United States exhibit.

www.ourdocuments.gov/doc.php?flash=true&doc=3
Our Documents: Articles of Confederation
This site features the engrossed copy of the Articles of Confederation.

Index